ALL GOOD THINGS

written and illustrated

by

Jennifer Shear

*

Second Edition

The sun and the moon
and the stars at night
all things in the heavens
and the dark and the light.

The rain that falls down
from up in the sky,

The wind that blows
and the clouds up high.

Great blue oceans
around all the land,

Streches of desert
all covered with sand.

Big green forests
full of tall trees,

Wide open fields
as far as one sees.

Huge snowy peaks
on mountains so tall,

Far reaching meadows
where grass covers all.

Trees with branches
covered in leaves,

Flowers and blooms
and blossoms for bees.

The birds in the sky
with wings to soar,

The beasts on the ground
that growl and roar.

All of the creatures,
the great and the small,

Everything living
He made it all.

He made our family
with his great hands,

He made all the people that live in the lands.

He also made you
and he even made me,

He made all that was
and that is to be.

www.ingramcontent.com/pod-product-compliance
Lightning Source LLC
Chambersburg PA
CBHW041244040426
42445CB00005B/141